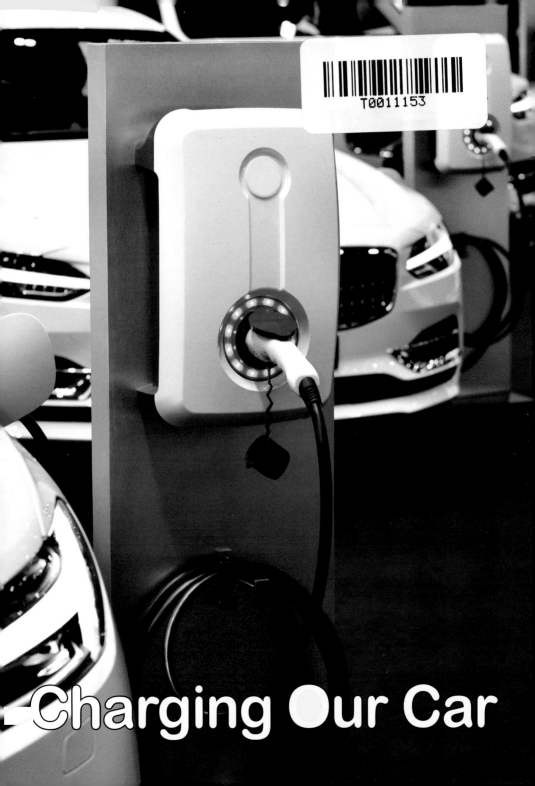

Charging Our Car

Here is our car.

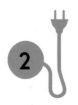

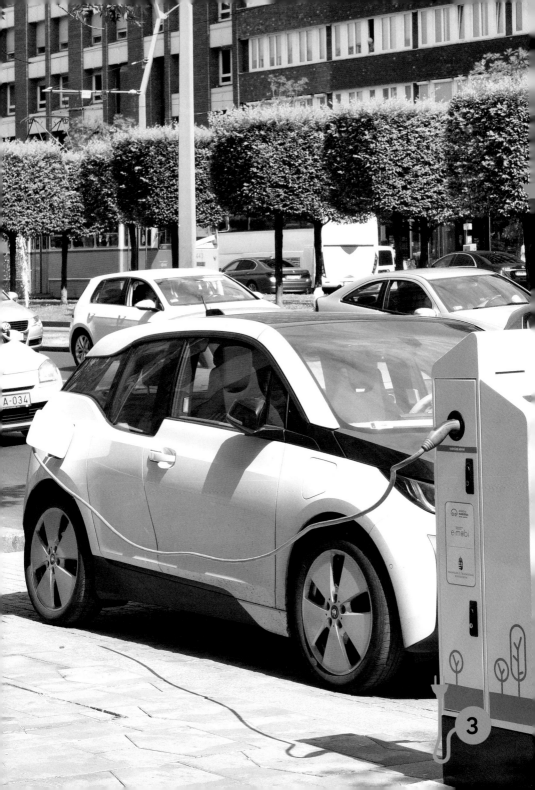

Electricity will make our car go.

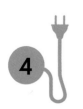

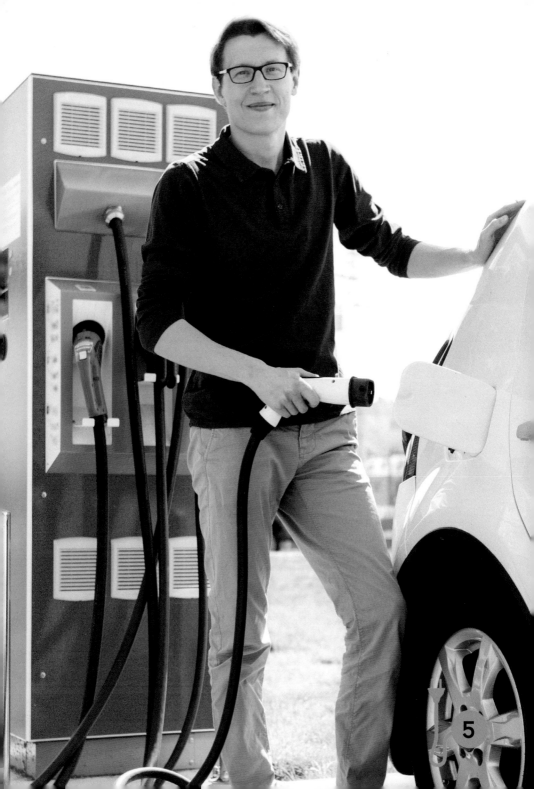

Look at this.

The electricity will go in here.

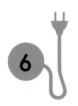

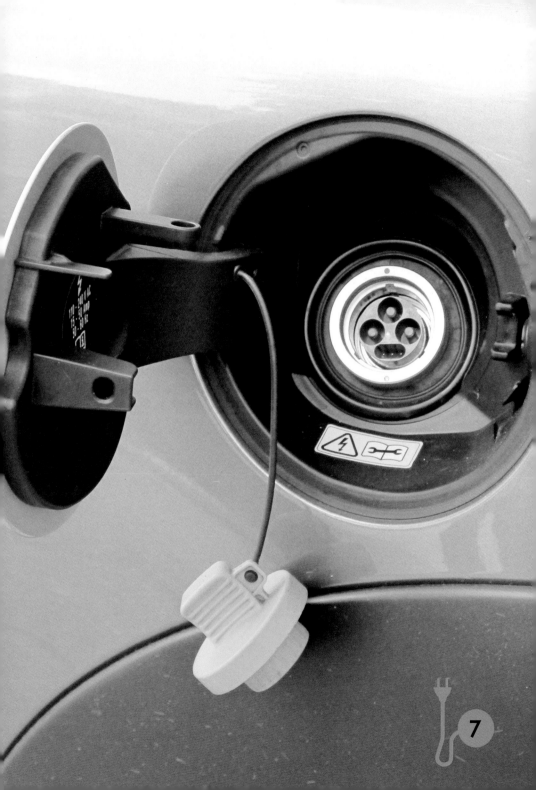

The electricity will make our car go and go.

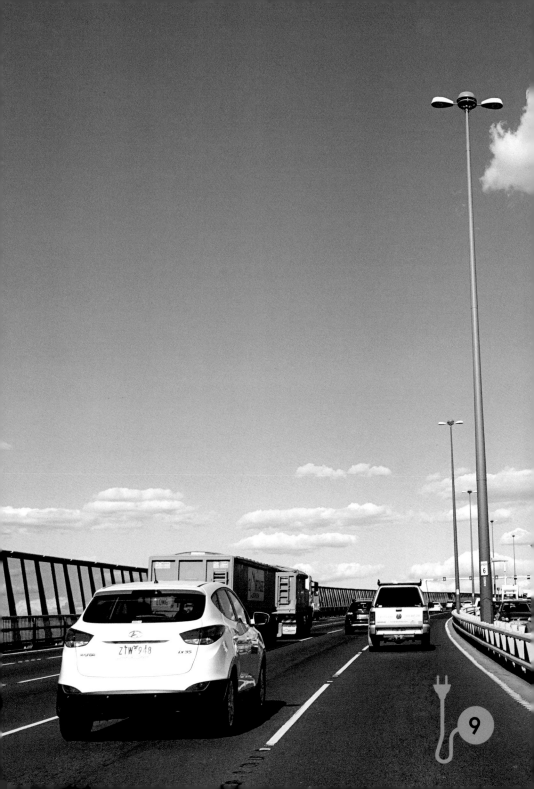

Our car can go here.

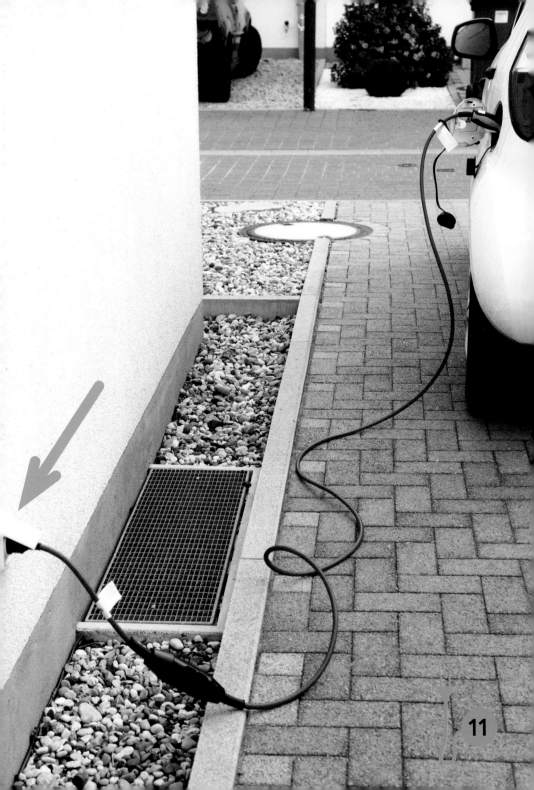

Our car can go here.

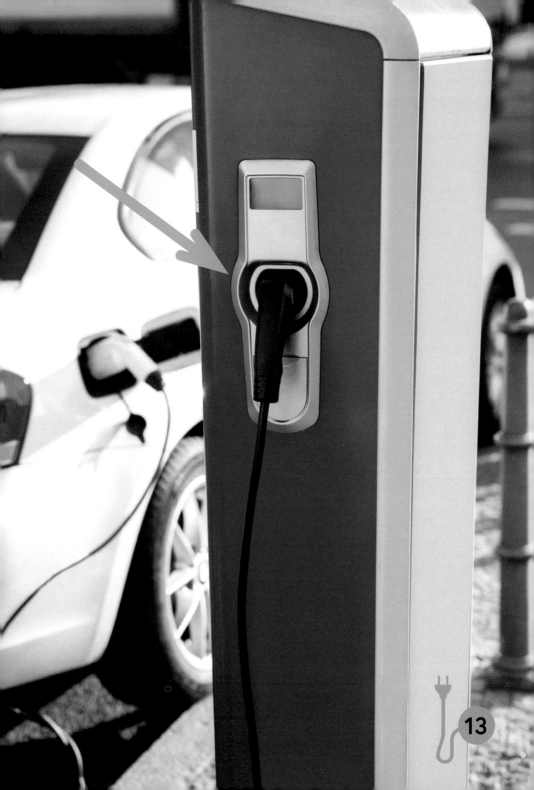

Our car can go here too.

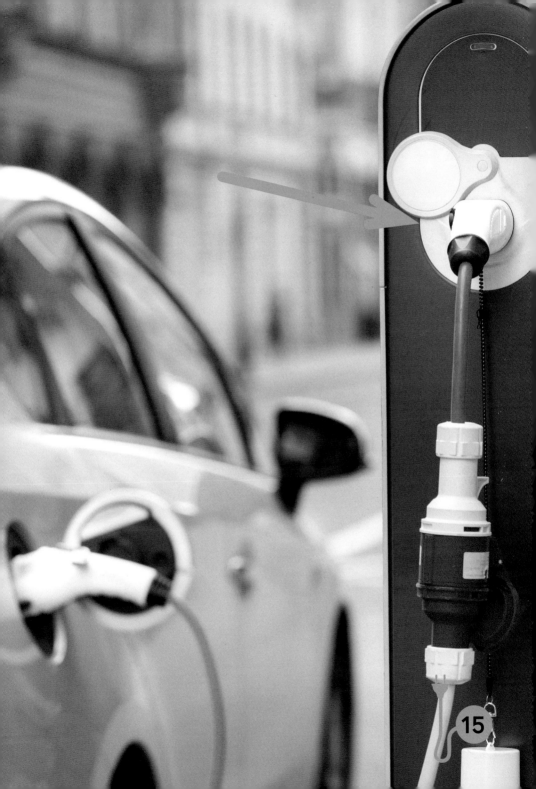

Away we go!

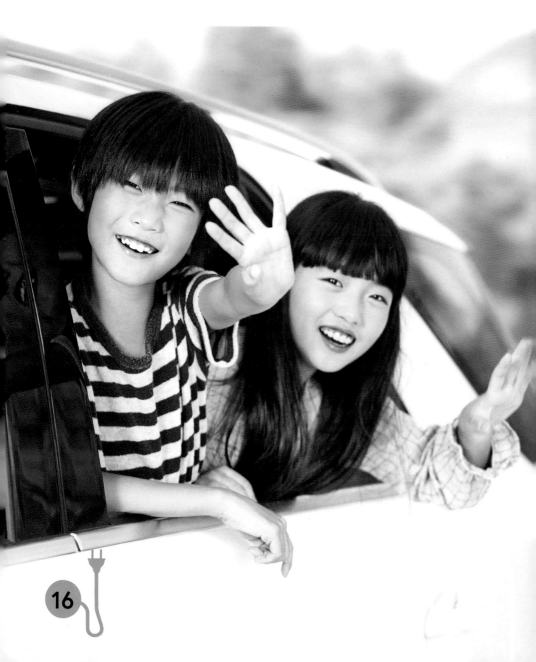